# The Eventpreneur Handbook.

...a guide for good service delivery!!!

Mayowa Oloyede

Foreword by **Funke Bucknor-Obruthe**

# DISCLAIMER

The information herein present in this report solely and fully represents the views of the author as of the date of publication. Any omission, or potential misrepresentation of, any peoples or companies, is entirely unintentional. As a result of changing information, conditions or contexts, this author reserves the right to alter content at their sole discretion impunity.

The report is for informational purposes only and while every attempt has been made to verify the information contained herein, the author assumes no responsibility for errors, inaccuracies, and omissions. Each person has unique needs and this book cannot take these individual differences into account. This book is copyright © 2017 with all rights reserved. It is illegal to copy, distribute, or create derivative works from this book in whole or in part. No part of this may be reproduced or transmitted in any form whatsoever, electronic, or mechanical, including photocopying, recording, or by any informational storage or retrieval system without expressed written, dated and signed permission from the author.

www.havilahdecor.com.

havilahtop@gmail.com.

# FORWARD

I have read it....

...very well done....

This book is very easy to read and most of all very insightful. It is also full of humor and it reflected the growing needs of the industry. It is both witty and educative.

For a new, aspiring and budding event planner this is a must read!

For established planners and designers, this is a major refresher course!

I recommend you buy, buy, buy and buy this book.

**Funke Bucknor-Obruthe**

CEO, Zapphaire Events.

## ACKNOWLEDGEMENT

My gratitude goes to God, the giver of life as well as to my wife, Daughter, Parents and Siblings etc, for their understanding while putting this piece together.

I cannot go without appreciating these CEOs and Event giants: Funke Buknor-Obruthe (Zapphaire Events); Bimbola Okutinyang (Bims Living Gardens); Motunrayo Laditan (Goldenhands Events) and Ted Thompson (Touch By Touch).

To PEPVAN (Professional Event Planners and Vendors Association of Nigeria), for the support for far – thanks a bunch!

Thank you all!

*The Eventpreneur Handbook*

...a guide for good service delivery!!!

# TABLE OF CONTENTS

DISCLAIMER

Forward

Acknowledgment

Introduction

Chapter 1:   Event Planning Checklist.

Chapter 2:   Event Planning and Management – The Facts.

Chapter 3:   The Event Management Nitty gritty.

Chapter 4:   Event Planning: The Worst and The Best.

Chapter 5:   Event Planning As A Business.

Chapter 6:   Event Coordination.

Chapter 7:   How To Stay Ahead of Competition.

Chapter 8:   Branding.

Chapter 9:   Event Agreement Form.

Chapter 10:  ...on The Final Analysis...

# Introduction

Event management practice is a great and wonderful experience, irrespective of whether it is your party, a corporate event billed for family and friends, or weddings and other more formal engagements.

Over the years, organisations have used events to deliver all sorts of messages, do Product launch, awareness etc. To their people; to potential clients; to shareholders as well as the multitude of other stakeholders relevant to their businesses in time and space.

Today, there is an upwardly mobile and powerful industry in full-scale development. Managing events, large or small are inspiring, memorable and with unlimited joy and satisfaction if planned properly and this is the goal of all event planners and vendors everywhere and a vital component of every single managed event is where event safety has the highest priority!

It's a tough job, as you would all agree with me, but it is very fulfilling and rewarding too! It can make a world of difference to the people, persons and parties involved who will greatly appreciate your kindness and monumental efforts in organizing their birthday, anniversary, wedding, birthday or other celebration or event.

Successful events are delivered by detailed planning, careful organization, and most importantly listening to the client. Hands on practical experience makes a huge difference in delivering successful events every time. Most event planners and vendors had obtained degrees in talking about all what they want to do with their clients BUT fail to put in for a Diploma course in developing their listening qualities and abilities in the school of life. Talkers aren't leaders but listeners- Learn to have good listening qualities so you would not be boring to your clients!

Money isn't everything! Even the brightest and best teams who work in the corporate event arena will flounder - big budget or not - unless they are organized and experienced in delivering what is needed to the highest possible standards of the clients. Many of the excellent event planners and vendors out there started from humble beginnings, the likes of Havilah Décor, Zapphire Events, Rostal Flowers, Bims Living Gardens, Goldenhands Events, Sapphires, Box 18 Media, One Media, B&B Ties, Just Flowers etc.

While looking around, majority of the planners and vendors have been able to deliver quality work consistently, over and over again and again coupled with the hands-on experience that only comes from being there as an event delivery takes place.

Few can combine experience, expertise and maintain the personal touch that is so vital - and rare - these days. Sure, there will always be a few hiccups - and the best event management teams will always seek to learn from these as they grow. The very best in the event management industry are particularly clear on how they go about ensuring that any event is delivered with just one simple outcome in mind and that the client is to be at the very least fully satisfied and even better, they will be thoroughly delighted with what they experience from their providers. One key to a successful event will be the capacity of any planner or vendor to have a clear understanding of the expectations, specifications and explanations of the client(s).

However, event management practice is the process of actions taken by which an event is planned, got ready in advance, and successfully produced with an understanding crop of team mates and unparalleled coordination per excellence! With the increasing importance of entertainment, event management as a business and career is gaining great momentum. Want to know more?

*Let's roll it!!!*

## Self-Assessment

What is it that makes one person succeed in the events industry while another fails? There is no one stereotype of a successful special events entrepreneur, but certain common characteristics can be found in those who succeed. For example, they are invariably hardworking, determined, resourceful, and capable of honest selfappraisal. Starting your own special events business is risky, and you need to be clear on whether it is the best choice for you.

You may already be working in the special events industry, but turning your skill into a business is a very different venture. Examining both your strengths and your weaknesses gives you the chance to remedy the factors that may impede your success. If you don't manage time well, don't like to work alone, and dislike making decisions, starting your own events business may not be appropriate — unless you are willing to work on your shortcomings. You don't have to be perfect, but you do need to recognize and acknowledge your strengths and weaknesses before investing time and money in a business.

A passion to succeed, an eagerness to learn, and an acceptance of responsibility can overcome any weaknesses. The value of any quiz, test, or questionnaire lies in that it can help you identify your strengths and admit your weaknesses. Look on this self-appraisal as an important first step in your journey to starting and running a successful special events business. You are capable of capitalizing on your strengths and compensating for your weaknesses as long as you know what they are and if your desire to do so is powerful enough. Once you have determined that starting a special events business is the right venture for you, take some time to test your ability to create special events.

Determining Your Market Once you have decided on whether or not this field is right for you, your next step is to determine your market or area of specialty. Is there a big enough market waiting to hire you to produce their special events? Make certain you discover this before you risk time and money on starting a business.

Many start-up operations are established solely on instinct and optimism. The enthusiastic new business owner may have only a vague idea about who his or her clients are or, indeed, whether or not there will be any clients at all. Operating on blind faith, such people are relying on plain old luck to see them through, and sometimes, it takes just that. However, while every business needs a little luck now and then, banking on it is hazardous to the long-term health of your enterprise. The special events industry is so vast that the event organizer is not limited to just one market segment.

**Market Research**

Your market is that segment of the population that could potentially use your service. Finding out who they are and what they want is called market research. This research will provide you with the data you need to help identify your potential clients and determine how to reach them. Conducting thorough market research is the foundation of any successful business.

# Chapter 1
# Event Planning Checklist

## *Questions To Ask Your Clients*

With many prospective clients, the consultation meeting is your first face to face interaction. This means it's also your first opportunity to make a good impression. Perhaps most importantly, client consultations are your chance to ask questions, get the details you need, and communicate with the client about each other's expectations. Are you worried that you'll forget what questions to ask once you're face to face? Make a list! There's no harm in bringing a questionnaire sheet or a tablet with you as a prompt.

When you're creating your list, make sure to include these 12 key questions!

### What kind of event is this? What is the purpose of the event?

This one seems like common sense, but ask it anyway! If you're going to plan a good, detailed, and enjoyable event, you need to know what you're working with. Hearing the purpose of the event described in the client's own words can give insight into their personality, style, and expectations.

**Do you have a prospective date?**

You need to know how long you have to plan the event so you can build a timeline and prioritize tasks. You also need to know whether planning that event within that timeframe is realistic.

**What is the location of your event?**

Will the event be in your current city, or does it require travel? The answer to this question could change how you approach planning, the amount of the estimate you give the client, or perhaps even whether you choose to work together.

**Have you already chosen a venue?**

If the venue is set, you'll have a starting point for the planning. If the venue hasn't been chosen yet, you'll be responsible for helping your client make that choice. As you can imagine, this will affect your planning timeline!

**How many guests are on your guest list?**

The earlier you know the size and scope of the event, the better. Countless other elements of the planning process depend on how many people will be in attendance. If the client hasn't determined the size of the guest list yet, this will be another important element for you to help them with quickly once you sign the contract.

## Are there any guests of honor?

Considering a guest of honor right from the beginning helps you focus your planning process. Who should be the center of attention? What are they celebrating? Make sure the event caters to that person's preferences as well as your actual client.

## Will the event involve any special features (e.g. a meal, guest speakers, live entertainment, etc)?

Not every event involves dinner and a show, but you'll need to know as soon as possible if it does! Hiring caterers, coordinating guest speakers, and booking live entertainment will make up a significant portion of your planning process if those elements are included in the event. List the top 3 most important factors that will make this event a success.

Get to know your client's top priorities. Which elements of the event do they want you to spend the most time and money on? You'll need to pay particular attention to these details in order for the event to be considered a success in your client's mind.

## Are there any elements you do not want at the event?

Different clients enjoy different activities, entertainment, and kinds of events.

Don't assume that new clients will have "cookie cutter" preferences and try not to rely on a standard event template. Asking them what they do want is essential, but asking them what they don't want can tell you even more about their expectations and personality.

**What kind of atmosphere would you like the event to have? Do you have a specific theme, style, or central color scheme in mind?**

This question gives insight into the kind of event you're planning and also the kind of client you're dealing with. Talking about themes and style immediately sets the tone for how you'll move forward if you decide to work together. If they haven't decided yet, you'll have a better idea of the scope of work involved on your end.

**What would you most like to hear guests say about the event when it's finished?**

This question is a great way to uncover your client's expectations without putting them on the spot and demanding that they list their expectations!

**What is your budget for the event (overall and per person)?**

Getting the details about the client's budget might be the most important part of the entire consultation meeting. You need to know whether the client can afford your services, whether the event they're prepared to pay for is within your abilities, and whether their expectation is realistic within that budget.

**Ask yourself questions too!**

Towards the end of the consultation meeting, silently ask yourself a few questions as well:

**Do you feel unclear about anything?**

**Do you have all of the details you need to move forward?**

> How are you and the potential client "meshing"? Do you feel comfortable about the idea of signing a contract with them? If the answer to any of these questions is "No", then you should seek clarification, ask them more questions, or evaluate whether this partnership is the best thing for you. If the answer is "Yes", then you're good to go!

Do you wish to plan events around product launch, conferences, seminars, birthdays, weddings, house warming, etc.? If so, check out these few practices of successful event planners and vendors. It's easy to dismiss these points thinking they're trivial. The steps below will teach you what should be put in your package and be check listed as soon as possible while planning for any event, going for any event and executing any event, give some suggestions to troubleshoot problems, and with careful planning, avoid them all together.

- **Back To The Basics...**

- ***Snapshoot the Purpose and Objectives of the Event:*** This rather seems a little too logical, but you need to get these down in permanent ink in order to know what is the *best size of venue, the right budget, the nature of presentations, amount (or type) of guests, and what strategies to employ for your specific event.* So what's your ideal outcome? What do you want to get done?

    - Once you figure out what you're doing (celebrating, fundraising, educating, product launch, selling, proposing, etc.), **think about "why" you're doing it**. Knowing fully well that your motivations can help give you focus and enough accelerated drive firing on all cylinders.

    - Having a few objectives can also help align you in the direction you need to be going. You can't keep trying to reach a goal that hasn't been set! When you have ***$5404*** and you're aiming for ***$4865*** that goal can push you through to the finish line.

    - Have a crystal clear purpose for the event. Have you attended a seminar where the topic was too broad, and the speakers seemed to talk all around the topic in a disconnected fashion? That's what happens when you lack clarity of purpose about the event.

- Is the event meant to be a strategic planning retreat for top management? Is it a seminar to bring medical professionals up-to-date on developments in a specialized field?

- If it is a product launch, exactly what outcome is the event expected to achieve? Only when you and your team know the core objectives can you organize a focused event that meets those goals.

- **Have you picked the date and time?** This is one of the most important factors in your event planning practice. Pick a date and time no one can make and it doesn't even matter how great an event you have planned. And pick a date and time that's too far into the future -- or coming up too soon -- and your guests will either forget about it or already have plans.

- Ideally, you want to let your guests know about two months, two weeks or two days out. That gives them a good amount of time to not yet have plans and a good timeline for inviting them and reminding them once or twice before the time actually comes. So have your event be a few weeks into the future minimum, if you can swing it.

- **This time, you have to handpick your venue...**

Now that you have a good idea of what you're doing

and when you're doing it, you can start thinking about venues and approaching potential ones with a date and things you'll need. What kind of building do you want to host in and how will the space be managed? Are the guests to be sitting on chairs in rows, at tables – Banquet, Classroom, Theatre format, etc or on picnic rugs in the open? Will the weather pose a problem? Will there need to be room for dancing, speaker's podium or a stage, backdrop, Aisle, high table, etc? If so, plan to ensure the event space or hall is large enough to accommodate these.

- It is always best to visit the site in advance as I normally do except it is too far away. But if within my state or not too far away, I do visit. If far away, (I could hear this question from the right Ventricle of your heart…lol) what I do is to oblige my client(s) to help snap or give me enough details of what could be so helpful for me in planning and would draw myself a map of the area for easy navigation of guests. This map can be used as a *"battle plan"* and allows you to sketch and allocate table space, service routes for food service, disabled access if required and exit routes, as well as how you will get the equipment into place. You should also mark where the power generator (if required), external equipment such Chiller, ice maker, Barbecue, Caterer (etc.) will be, as well as where power points and cables will be (which may be covered discreetly with a rug), DJ, Band, Ushers, etc and other safety hazards to address.

- **Are legal and local government approvals required?** In most instances approvals are required for a bar, but also for excessive noise, vehicle access and parking, building large enclosures such as a pavilion and other needs.

- **Determine the guests to invite**... how? You ask?

  How many people can your planned budget and venue handle? Some events are strictly ticket entry or invitation only, so it is easier to plan, but many events will have late comers, gate crashers...lol, "I hear I branch" guests or extras such as children, well wishers or friends. And keep in mind that the more guests you have, the more crew you need, too. As this can be the biggest logistical problem it's always wise to ensure there is adequate room for all people to move around at the event hall or space.

- **Be decisive on a reliable budget.** You know what? Hopefully you have a few people you can lean on to discuss together with you on how much money you'll need for this event. Are you paying any staff? Renting equipment and your venue? Supplying food and drinks? Publishing pamphlets or postcards? Settle on a number that seems doable and cater your plan to it. You don't want to wind up paying out of your own pockets for this if you don't have to.

- You may be in a situation where you can get sponsorships or donations, but most of us aren't so lucky. If you don't foresee any more funds coming in, it's imperative that you cut corners (I mean, reduce your cost by all means whatsoever) when need be. Instead of having a catering team, form a Ajah or a "bring-a-plate" function (catering is minimal, but you will need to provide a food table, Cooler, Ice Chess yourself). Instead of hiring a photographer, go around and take photos yourself. Get creative where need be! Lol.

- **Read the fine print, know all details:** As an event planner, you may be exposing yourself to serious financial and another risk if you are not entirely familiar with all aspects of the event. That includes all contracts you sign, all written instructions, orders and more. Since you are the event planner, you're expected to be the expert on all these areas.

- **Get functional, dynamic and Proactive Team mates...**

Organize your Think Thank team (even if they are friends and relatives or other volunteers) to handle different, relevant sections, even if you're not professionally running an event, but running a small family event. Good event management in a big scale is about organising people to be in charge of individual areas of the event and making sure everyone knows what the plan is all about.

- Your crew or team mates needs just as much advanced notice as the teams you're hiring and your guests. Assign them duties and responsibilities as soon as possible, giving them preference if you can. And try to have a few people on standby -- there are always a few flakes in every bunch.

- **What about the Agenda?**

    No more planning can happen until you know just what's going to happen at your event. When are the speakers speaking? Are there games, activities, or presentations that should be scheduled? How much time will the guests need to eat, talk, play, relax etc? Work out a fairly detailed timeline for the day's activities.

- Always leave a little breathing space for "expansion and compression"! No event will be exactly as you planned, down to the minute. People run late, speeches take a bit longer than expected, the line for the buffet doesn't follow along, you name it. So while you need a good idea of what's happening, understand that it is for organizational purposes and nothing is written in stone...

- **Ensure that information flows freely across your team...**

You rarely do event planning or engage in event practice in isolation. You'll almost always have a team of people to whom you have delegated various responsibilities for. It's very easy to make assumptions that everyone knows what the event is all about and how what they are doing ties in with what everyone else is doing. Both assumptions can be totally incorrect.

- At the very beginning of the event planning practice by any planner or vendor, take the time to share your event or client's objective and your overall plan for executing it with every single one of your team members. It's best to get them all together to do this explaining. On an ongoing basis, have regular meetings to assess the progress so that everyone is aware of all aspects of the event.

- **Make sure all Speakers and all other performers are confirmed asap...**

    Sometimes, you come across events where the main speaker delivers his message wonderfully well, except that what he said had nothing to do with the purpose of the event! Network with other event planners, find out who would be a good speaker for the event you're planning. Someone might be an excellent speaker for one event, but not necessarily for another. Ask the speaker for references. Find out as much as you can from those references. Ask them how many times they've heard him speak. What did they like about his performance? What did they not like? Do they have any particular relationship with the speaker (which might colour their opinion)

- **Don't just double check, Triple-check everything!!!**

    This is one of the most useful planning mottos you can think of. Someone may have promised you three months ago that they'll serve exotic Chinese snacks and high tea. Closer to event date but sufficiently in advance, check again to make sure they remember the commitments made to you if you don't want to mess yourself up big time. They have many other things to do and may have completely forgotten what they said months ago!

    I would say more later, just continue with the flow…

# Chapter 2

# Event Planning and Management- The Facts

The event planning industry is host to numerous job titles and job descriptions. Event planner. Meeting planner. Event Coordinator. Convention planner. Event manager. The list seems endless. As the industry grows, so does the list of job functions. While job growth is always a good thing, the range of event planning job functions and event management job titles can be terribly confusing to those starting out in the industry.

These are most probably similar in analogy to planning a typical birthday party, where the preparations need to be set up in the most effective ways. However, there are more intimate details in event management practice that need to be paid close attention to. It is equally frustrating for seasoned professionals faced with clients who misunderstand the services offered.

Nowadays, the term **Event management** seems to refer to a comfortable yet sophisticated and chic profession. And in actual sense, some consequences and accountabilities are attached to this classy title of being a service provider.

Concepts have to be visualized, planned, budgeted, and executed in events that are often highly regarded such as fashion or beauty shows, concerts, corporate seminars, exhibitions, wedding celebrations, theme parties, product launching, etc.

What is good about this career and its gaining popularity is the minimal requirement for financial investments, yet it allows the planner to be independent and flexible. Personal traits, character, and attitude are of more importance in event planning. The planner of events must possess a real passion in holding or conducting affairs. They need to be organized and able to work in flexible and often extended hours. Although this exciting career among the younger generation may have been seen as a sensational one, it also demands a substantial amount of hard work and effort.

Perfection is a major quality that must be achieved in any event management and therefore requires a great quantity of patience, good communication skills, and comprehension to be practiced by an *event manager*. Duties must be discharged with efficiency. Challenges must be confidently faced, and situations must be given due attention and reaction. Team spirit, leadership, and organizational skills are as well required in event planning practice. Every detail no matter how small, must be paid close attention to.

There are also courses available to be taken by anyone who decides on taking a career in event planning. Eligibility courses usually require to have a bachelor's degree in any discipline, but most preferred are management-related fields, social sciences, liberal arts, and humanities.

However, these terms, "**Event management**" and "**Event planning**" are frequently tossed around interchangeably even though they are two very different things. Quite simply, planning and managing are not the same. While the skill sets of these two functions do overlap, they are two distinct functions. This creates problems for those dealing with clients who mistakenly think they need an event manager when what they need is an event planner. And for those clients who are under the impression that all event managers also handle event planning. So let's clear up the confusion because it is important that you and your clients have the same understanding.

## Event Management vs. Event Planning

### Event Planning

Let's start with event planning. The key operative word here is *planning*. All events – from bridal showers to milestone birthday celebrations to big corporate gatherings – begin with a plan of some sort. The initial discussions with clients regarding event ideas, themes, desirable dates and budget guidelines are all part of the event planning process.

Be aware that event planning starts at the beginning, from the very early stages of concept and continues all the way until the actual event takes place. And, honestly, for a few weeks after the event as event planners wrap up details and handle follow up items.

Event planning involves working closely with the client to design an event that reflects the client's vision of the gathering and meets the event's objective. Clients who hire an event planner hire someone to plan all aspects of the event, including the related details and action items, and to see that event through until its completion.

Event planning responsibilities can include but are not limited to:

- Selecting an overall theme for the event
- Developing a budget
- Selecting a venue
- Negotiating hotel contracts
- Hiring outside vendors
- Planning the menu
- Hiring a caterer
- Arranging for guest speakers or entertainment
- Coordinating transportation
- Choosing the color scheme
- Developing invitations etc

Event planning is everything that goes into putting together an event. This function falls under the larger umbrella of event management.

Do you understand? Okay, let's go...

**Event Management**

As we all know that every type of event is made up of numerous parts that fit together like pieces of a puzzle. All of those pieces ultimately come together to create an event. Successful events have all of those related pieces coming together at the right time and the right place, smoothly and efficiently and according to plan.

This process is called ***event management***. It is, in simple terms, project management of the event itself.

Event management involves creating, coordinating and managing all the different components of an event as well as the teams of people responsible for each aspect. Some aspects of event management may include but are not limited to:

- Reserving a location for an event
- Coordinating outside vendors
- Developing parking plan
- Designing emergency contingency plans
- Ensuring compliance with health and safety

standards

- Managing staff responsible for each function
- Overseeing execution of event
- Monitoring of the event
- Resolving event situations on site

**Event Managers and Event Planners' Work**

To clearly define these two functions is challenging because, not only are they closely related, the responsibilities often overlap. Individual event planners may offer event management services and event managers may also offer event planning. It all depends upon the individual planner or corporate event management team, the venue, and the event itself.

It is important to understand the differences between the two and to determine which services you will provide. If, for example, you offer event planning services for a large scale event, you will work with an event manager who will coordinate your services with those of the catering manager, the audio visual team, baker, etc. Define your role and the services you will provide and clearly communicate these to prospective clients to avoid any confusion during the planning process.

However, individuals who are of interest simply have to

finish these courses that are offered by some established Event Planning/Management Companies and some principles that include public relations, organizational development, communication and implementation are inculcated in them.

Training and experience also contribute in becoming an adept and qualified *event manager*. While at school, the aspirant may work as an event staff personnel for sporting festivals and leagues. If there are local music shows to be held, assist in the preparation. Internships also play a major role in molding a successful planner. Upon completion of qualifying courses, the event planner can join established companies in event planning, or they may choose to set up and start their own business. Employment is available from corporate and public sectors, government agencies, tourist agencies, hotels, banks and other financial institutions, private consultancy firms, etc.

# Chapter 3

# The Event Management Nitty Gritty...

- ## Getting Set

• *Be available to send out invitations on time.* This is because how else will people know to come?! You gotta send them invites! And this isn't something you should scrimp on, either. Your invitation is the face of your event. The first impression people get of what to expect and if they should even come. It's gotta be good.

- *Consider your invitations, type and format – a postcard, flyers, etc.* But also you can go paperless: email, newsletters, Facebook, Twitter, and sites like Eventbrite that serve as invitations, guest trackers, and a calendar.

**N.B**. If you're trying to get as many people to come as possible, definitely use Facebook and Twitter. If you're trying to keep it to VIPs only, *avoid these* *platforms*. That's just asking for trouble.

## Keep Track

- You'll need a headcount to know just how much and what you all need, so keep track! It probably won't be the number that actually shows up, but it should give you a general idea. Websites designed for event managing can help you do this -- but so can Facebook and an Excel spreadsheet.

## Be In Charge

- Will you need to find, hire, book or delegate photographers, builders, designers and decorators, guest speakers, sponsors, entertainers or bands, officiates or clergy, dancing partners or demonstrations? It is wise to include them in catering and seating calculations so that a meal and a table place is provided for them if appropriate or required, too.

Are food and beverages provided? If so, know who will be on the team to look after the cooking, serving and cleaning. What type of food do you need to serve? Are there likely to be guests with allergies, vegetarian or vegan needs, diabetics, religious needs such as halal or kosher, gluten-free, (etc)? And will there be infants, young children or the aged or injured who cannot eat solid foods?

- Are entertainment and logistics organised? This part might be delivery of music equipment, pavilions or tents and decorative effects or stage management you will need, such as a microphone and amplifiers, lighting, power outlets, projectors and screens for slideshows, smoke machines or other stage magic effects such as mirrors, banners and corporate signage, etc.

- If you subcontract a company to be entertainers, consult with them to ensure they are able to supply and set-up their own equipment as well as where the stage and service sections will be on the site and what the schedule will be. This way you can find out what you may need to do to assist them.

- Caterers, florists, entertainers and other important people appreciate as much time as possible to plan, as it is typically more expensive to obtain goods and staff for high urgency requests. The other advantage is should they not be able to keep your appointment, you have some time still to find an alternative.

- Find someone who will be the master of ceremonies (MC). The MC doesn't always organise the event entirely, but they do host the event. It is usually a member of the party, who will organise speeches, announce events such as the meal courses, dancing, notable guests or entertainment. Liaise with this person often and keep them up-to-date. If they're any good, they'll be very helpful. Sometimes you may have to be the MC, in which case the job becomes much harder as you will need to keep working until it's all over. It then becomes important to set up your service team with their own group leaders so you can delegate most of the normal duties to them.

- ### Gather Your Pieces Together

  When you hire a team, check and "triple"-check that they're bringing the gear they need. In some cases, they may just be providing you bodies or goods and leaving it at that; you may need to source the equipment separately. It can be rented, bought, or even borrowed from your extensive social network. Go through your checklist from napkins to PA systems to extension cords.

- Decorations are a huge part of any event. Table linens, flowers, gifts, candles, balloons, banners or backdrops for photography, red carpets, (etc) should always be sourced well in advance.

### Cover Your Base

- One thing many rookies forget are the finer points of the facilities, event specs and details, Décor props,

Ushers, special music, interludes, interjections etc. Are there enough so flaws would not be exposed? Other examples are toilets accessories, bathrooms, car parking spaces, wheelchair access ramps, changing rooms, storage rooms and kitchen space, waste disposal bins, wine coolers, power access, etc. These are obstacles that are only workable if you foresee them well in advance.

- *Also think outside of your event*: will transport and accommodation be required for international or out-of-town guests or delegates at hotels, as well as bookings and space made for their transport to get them to and from the event?

## Who Are You Dealing With? 

Understanding the social hierarchy of your event -- if it's not truly yours -- is integral to knowing how to handle any situation. As it is essential that the client has confidence in you, you will need to find out:

- *Who the key guests are*—this is usually straightforward when it is a celebration event—such as the bride and groom. The client is not always the key guest/s but may be part of their group, or not present at all.

- *Who the host guests are*—these people often act as hosts at their own tables and tend to be good socializes and motivators of guests. These people are useful to keep a convivial atmosphere and strike up a conversation if things turn quiet, encourage people to dance or to introduce people to other guests to make new friendships. These people should be reliable but are generally useful to know as they will keep you informed, may step in and be a guest speaker or MC for you in an emergency and these are the people overall who make the event flow the smoothest at the front line.

- *Who the peacemakers are*. You should be aware at all times who these key people are as you need to advise them of issues and involve them in the handling of issues and disputes where appropriate. This will generally be the head of the family, a caretaker, or head honchos or hired security.

- *Who the decision maker is*. For most cases it is yourself the *event manager*, but when you must consult guests and it is not appropriate to involve the key guests (as they typically will be occupied being good hosts), find out who you should consult in an emergency. Ultimately it would be the person who pays the bill if you're charging for your services, or whosoever you may deem as "the client" as the person having the final say on the matter.

## Getting Closer To The Event Day

- Get familiar with the venue. Well before the event, it's a good idea to scope out your venue and figure out how everything will be set up with every stakeholder. You may need to make additional arrangements to accommodate the floor plan -- extension cords, lighting, etc. And if it's hard to find for you, it'll probably be hard to find for your guests, so be sure to take that into account, too!

- It is up to you, map out where everything will go and when. If there isn't room for it, it needs to go. Talk to the venue's manager about what help they are willing and able to pitch in and if there are special number you need to have especially in the case of emergency.

- Check in with all teams before the event, it's important to have all your ducks in a row and all your eggs in a basket...lol! Be sure to provide clear instructions to your crew on how to get to the site and give them your number or preferably a business card with contacts to call if they need directions. Does anybody have any questions? No? And break!

- Consider getting them badges or a little party favor to make them feel part of the event and to remember it by. And make sure they stay fed and watered so they won't be hustling for what is not! Always think of your team as resources you want to be able to use in the future.

Make sure everyone is comfortable with their duties. Some people may not be willing to vocalize this, so read them if at all possible. Do they seem sure and confident? If not, reassure them, go over their duties, and ask them a few basic questions. When in doubt, pair them with a more able partner.

Make a checklist. As your service providers file in, you'll know what goods, what equipment, and what props are missing.

- Avoid last-minute changes. Is it likely there will be frequent artistic changes? Weddings are infamous for clients making last minute design changes so it is wise to recommend to your clients a cut-off date for changes. Usually 1 week before the event is leaving it very close, but it gives the client some flexibility and avoids last minute changes coming too late to be practical or cost effective to implement.

- If it is simple, subtle or basic changes using already sourced decorations, then it is not unreasonable to accede to change requests. Be as accommodating as possible in what is usually a very emotionally anticipated event.

- Consider making kits for your team. Your crews are going to be working hard. In order to show them your appreciation and to keep them on top of their game, make them a kit to give at the top of the event. Bottles of water, granola bars, chocolates, little tokens of appreciation, whatever you see fit. It'll up morale from the get-go, too.

## Manager Indeed!!!

- Make sure everything is set. Be the first to arrive at the site to oversee the preparations. Make sure everyone files in accordingly and start making phone calls if not. Assist those who need assisting, direct those who need directed, and get out of the way when you need to. No injuries until after the event, please.

- You'll feel a little calmer if you make a To-Do list. Have a portion for your crew, a portion for hired out crews, a portion for decorations and basic set-up, and a portion for equipment. When all is checked off, that's when you have time to breathe. Then,

- Delegate. Do not be afraid to delegate. The main stressor when it comes to an event is time. To save it, all hands need to be on deck -- or different decks. If someone isn't being as useful as they could be, give them something better to do. It's your job. It's not you being bossy or overstepping your boundaries; it's you doing what you're supposed to do.

- When you delegate, be firm but polite! Say something like, *"Michelle, I need you over here right now to help out with the caterers or DJ or Ushers etc.*

*Thank you."* Your crew needs to jive together as much as the event does. Keep everything moving swimmingly by being the leader that you need to be.

- Be flexible. This means making sure that things are kept to schedule and assisting or having backup plans if it falls behind -- "and being okay with it". If you start stressing out, you'll lose your head. Nothing good will come of that. So when that speech runs ten minutes over and the speaker is ignoring your blatant distress signals or your attempt at feigning a stroke to create a diversion, relax. You'll just adjust the appetizer and no one will notice. Event intact.

• Things happen. They do. They have a bad habit of happening. There's no way you can predict everything every time and the sooner you accept this, the better.

A calm, collected *event manager/coordinator* can do wonders for any event; a strung-out, tense one cannot. So relax and go with the flow -- it'll all be over soon!

- Keep everyone updated. Check that guest numbers and needs are still correct on the day of the event and advise the service team of any changes at the earliest possible opportunity you should be the first set of eyes that notices if anything goes wrong.

    Consult with your clients to see how they are feeling; they may be excited, nervous, worried, bored or mentally drained or have some issue on their plate that in some cases you may soothe with understanding, some kind words and practical assistance. It is wise to use this time to rejuvenate the enthusiasm in guests and the team where appropriate.

- Be at your thing and game. Trust and respect your service team to look after themselves -- if you've given them a good base, they should be fine. Offer assistance if needed, but they should be experienced enough not to need any help at all. Here are a few things to keep in mind.

    - Act as a concierge or receptionist or usher at the beginning, meeting and greeting each guest (if appropriate) as they come. Hand over the reins to the MC when the event starts. The management role will be more active problem solving and ensuring all the back of house work such as food preparation and service runs to plan.

    - Keep an eye on the guests and keep contact with the MC often and discreetly in case they want (or need) to change plans.

    - Keep a respectful distance from the key guests - after all, the event is all about them - but be easily accessible by checking at appropriate moments how they feel the event is going, as well as any problems, requests or suggestions they may have.

- Refrain from making it known publicly that the event is being delayed because of certain guests (because the party will work that out on their own), but advise key hosts or members of the party that you have been made aware of the fact. Let them know what you intend to do, but allow the hosts to make a suggestion as they know the members of their party and what would be appropriate in the context.

- Maintain careful watch on the time in relation to speeches. If key guests are late, serve an additional appetizer (first course) and/or beverage early as this will prevent guests who came on time from becoming bored and will keep them occupied.

- For guests that are going to be delayed for more than is reasonable or possible (such as when serving food that simply cannot wait, such as Bread and Tea), start the event as planned and when the delayed guests arrive, start them at the next course of a meal (even if this is dessert).

- Organize an additional dance, game, speech or other form of entertainment (especially music), and ensure extra distractions, such as group or party photographs are done until they arrive and this back-up strategy should be considered the day in advance.

For guests deliberately arriving late, it should be seen as that guest's choice, not your fault as manager, so your duty is first to the guests that

are already present and to ensure they're looked after. In a nutshell, act as if there is no problem and carry on regardless.

Know how to handle food issues. This one is rare if you have planned things carefully, however accidents do happen (such as a guest or young child making a mess of a food table, or an accident in the kitchen). Early on you should be aware of the type of guests so you can take into account when and where food is displayed (such as for a buffet) and where such guests are seated.

- Any spillage for safety reasons must be cleaned up immediately, even if it means removing a red carpet or desired decor and furniture to be able to do so. If it is impossible to hide a stain without affecting the appearance or the integrity of the item (such as an antique), then removal is wise. If you have a spare, then use that; if not, move the existing furniture or decor subtly so it does not feel missing.

- A soft rope barrier, curtain or screen is recommended whenever you need to hide the food area (such as a buffet with chafing dishes, or when organizing a "reveal" of the next course), as certain guests may feel that if food is in the dining area, it is free-for-all, when they want -- which is not always the case.

- Unexpected vegetarians, those with food allergies, religious or special diets — no surprise should ever occur with proper planning — but guests occasionally do bring along additional family members, partners or close friends without advising you, especially if it's not a strict invitation-only event. This is usually easily resolved. Keep a headcount as guests arrive and when they arrive at the door, ask if there are any food requirements and advise the kitchen and service staff immediately.

- For large unexpected groups that are not gatecrashers, send a team member to the kitchen to take stock and, if necessary, drive out to collect more supplies. Kitchens typically over-cater to cover for accidents and more often there are more cancellations than unexpected guests. Limited portions can be stretched when you provide additional fillers, such as bread rolls, salad or vegetable portions, ingredients for which can be quickly sourced from local supermarkets.

- Know how to deal with children. It's wise to remember that many managers have made serious errors in underestimating the intelligence or forgetting the needs and desires of children at events, as they have the same needs and wants as adults - to have a good time and not be bored. Remember that their parents are also often offended if the event does not cater for their children. In practice, it is best to request an RSVP for every child that may come.

    - Young children (under 10) are best given food or snacks early as many dinner events have the meals start as late as 8pm, which is far later than most children are used to. Food provided should be fun and healthy but as special as the adult menu as parents appreciate special touches for their children - it makes their job easier so they can have fun as guests in their own right.

    - Over 10's usually are fine to be served adult food and portions, even if they don't eat all of it, but offer the children's menu to them (with their parent's permission) if they don't seem keen on the options. It has also been known for young adults 13-18 to often request the same food as youngsters, such as a hamburger and fries as opposed to more formal restaurant food and it has been a frequently used trick to re-brand the children's menu as an *"Alternative Menu"* for this age group of guests. It is very wise to play safe and discuss with key guests about your plans to keep the young and old engaged, well in advance of the date.

- A discrete area should be provided for mothers with young children for their needs such as toilet/bathroom breaks, breastfeeding (etc.), and a place for very young children to sleep in if they are tired.

• Know how to deal with rowdy or intoxicated guests, gate-crashers and other guest problems. Ideally this would never happen, but it does — family or corporate events both. Politics and drama often come out at events that, as an outsider, you would not be always aware of. Prepare yourself.

Ask the client or key guests before the event of the likelihood of such issues, or with selected hosting guests if it is not appropriate to discuss these issues with the key guests, so that way you can ensure that people are seated in places that will not cause issue. Enlist service staff or key-guests to act as unofficial monitors, to keep an eye out for issues and to step in when required. Strictly speaking, your duty is to ensure the event is smoothly run, but only where it is appropriate, and to stay out of issues that are a private concern. Therefore, you should be aware of who within the party are the "peacemakers" of the group.

- Gatecrashers are difficult. Plan using Bouncer who check all tickets, Invites and pass at the entrance.

- Know how to handle inclement weather. Sudden, unexpected rain can be common in parts of the country; likewise, a severe heat condition or a cold front can also pose a problem. While weather events are not usually an issue if you're indoors, being outside makes things difficult. If bad weather is expected, then consider moving the event location. If the event cannot be relocated or rescheduled, hire a large tent or pavilion (admittedly this can be pricey on short notice). Keeping an eye on weather developments as you go is important; very little can be done to salvage an event affected by weather, so make the best of what you have.

- Then, learn to congratulate yourself after the event. Most events tend to run themselves when they start, but all the hard work is the preparation that no-one sees. So pat yourself on the back because you deserve it! Okay, back to tearing it down. The job's not over yet!

After the event, arrange a time to meet and thank your client. It is always recommended to offer an appropriate and thoughtful gift to remember their time with you, as it is these small touches that make the experience richer and may make them recommend your services in future. If you gave a gift during the event, such as in a gift registry with the other guests, then a thoughtful after present such as flowers, a framed photograph of your favourite moment at their event (such as cutting the ribbon, or the climax of the show, or the award ceremony, or the wedding kiss, or blowing out the candles on a cake, etc), or some other gift may be appropriate.

- Clean up and get out! Just like my mom always say, "Leave it in the same condition you found it in," the same goes for your venue. Everything needs to be just like it was before you got there -- this is one business where you don't want to burn any bridges. So let your crew knows it's time to tear down and don't let them leave until all is taken care of. And you need to pitch in too!

    - This is nice, sure, but it also prevents you from being billed any more than you should be. Many places will tack on extra cleaning fees if they find any opportunity to do so. So make it as spic and span as possible to avoid the hidden costs.

    - Take note of this: Keep all your payments safe and thank all parties. You may need to arrange returning hired or borrowed equipment and later on consulting with the client about their experience. **Even if unpaid after the event**, thank them for the opportunity to have such a great experience to run an event with them. Can you get a business card of theirs?

- Thank your crew too! Thank all team members, especially sponsors and volunteers. You couldn't have done it without them!
Make sure all parties are paid (and all parties have paid up), file receipts, and get everyone taken care of. You should be one of the last ones out the door -- and make sure it's locked behind you.

# Chapter 4

# Event Planning: The Worst Job and the Best!!!

Event planners constantly like to hear about how we have the "the best job ever" and how other people "would love to have our job"! While this is nice to hear other people say, we all know that the event industry also has its downsides and that an event planner job isn't perfect.

Depending on your job within the event world you might get to meet interesting people, travel to beautiful places and enjoy experiences that some of your friends or family might envy. The perks can be really great, but the job is not without it's challenges.

If you are new to events, here are a few details about the less glamorous side of event management. Sometimes these items may make this job seem like a drag, but they can also be the best part!

**Long and Unpredictable Hours**

Most people see a full time job as working from 9am-7pm Monday through Friday, even Saturday to Sunday at times but that all goes out the window when you become an event professional. You will most likely be working nights, weekends and extended hours during and leading up to your event. It is not uncommon to hear of event planners putting in 100 hour weeks! While this isn't always the case, you need to be ready for the ups and downs of the event industry hours.

While it can be tough to work the long hours during an event, you will find that these are the days that you really bond with your event team and have fun working together! Make the most of the crazy long days and focus on bonding as a rock star team! There will be time to celebrate and relax once your event is completed.

**You Must Always Be Connected**

Answering calls in the middle of the night might not sound like something you would expect an event planner to do, but rest assured all of us have been there. You have to be on and ready to work no matter the time. From email to calls to managing social media you might find yourself unable to disconnect.

In between important events there will be moments where you are able to unplug, but during your busy periods clients, attendees, vendors and venues will all be vying for your attention. In order to keep everyone happy and things running smooth you must always be available to answer that important call/email/text.

The great part about being so connected is that this leaves many event planners with the ability to work from any destination or at any time. The flexibility of travel and not being chained to a desk all day is a huge perk that we get to enjoy in the event industry.

**Unhappy Customers**

Dealing with less than satisfied customers is a challenge in every industry, but for some reason event clients can take this to an entirely new level. Perhaps it is the pressure of the day and the many moving parts that go into an event, but if you get into this industry there will come a time where someone will be unhappy and you will hear about it. It is never fun to be reprimanded or given negative feedback, but you have to learn to take it with a grain of salt and use the feedback as motivation to improve in the future. We all make mistakes don't beat yourself up too much.

## High Levels of Stress

Being an event coordinator/planner constantly ranks as of the top-5 most stressful careers (yawn!). Stress can really take a toll on your body, mind and energy levels. Often times it can even lead to burnout and have some planners looking for a new career.

While stress can be tough to manage, event planners who can find a way to thrive under the pressure will really succeed in this industry. Use this stress as motivation to set yourself apart as someone who is calm, cool and collected when others might crumble. Part of the fun is event planning is thinking on your feet and adapting to every new situation. Make sure you are a proud event professional per excellence.

## Travel

While jet setting to a variety of destinations for jobs sounds like a dream, it can become very exhausting and lonely after the novelty wears off. We love our frequent flyer miles and venue points, but missing home and your normal daily routine can make even the best destination seem like a chore.

If you travel often for work, find ways to enjoy and embrace the experience. Travel can be so much fun and the places you get to see might be once in a lifetime destinations! To make it more enjoyable try tacking on a few extras days where you can actually soak in the destination outside of work, or bring a family member or friend along for the trip! When you are home, focus on maintaining your relationships and getting into your routine to make the most of your time off the road.

## Unpredictability

While we all take pride in planning every last detail, you never know what might happen at an event. Throughout your career you are sure to see and hear things that they don't teach you in school and you have to be ready to think on your feet. This can be a very difficult part of the job and lead to the stress and long hours mentioned above. Some days you might have a new hurdle to overcome and other days might bring a pleasant and positive surprise.

At the same time, this unpredictability is what makes an event management career so much fun! No day is ever the exact same and every event is like taking on a new adventure. You will always be learning new skills and meeting new people. Not many jobs or careers have this added perk.

Event planning can be a very tough job. There will be times that you wonder why you got into this career in the first place, but hopefully these moments are few and far between. More often than not the things that make the event planner job tough, can also be what make it so enjoyable. Take time to learn from each experience and challenge you encounter.

# Chapter 5

# Event Planning As a Business

The event planning industry is incredibly multi-faceted as you will all agree! It is unlike a lot of career where you're stuck in a cubicle doing the same work day in and day out, there are many levels to event planning that makes it one of the most flexible and fun businesses to be a part of.

There are several avenues to explore, especially, when deciding if this is the right career path for you. That's because there are so many different types of events that can be planned, leaving endless possibilities. That's a great thing because it leaves the door open to new opportunities!

If you want to know how to get started in event planning, the first step is simple...

**Hey! YOU HAVE TO START WITH YOURSELF**. Think about what kind of events you have attended and what you enjoyed the most about them. Was it the theme or type of event? Also, think about your passion. What inspires you and gets your creative juices flowing?

Maybe you've planned your events, everything from dinner parties to birthday parties. I'm sure you remember the satisfaction that you felt on the result. What event did you most enjoy planning and what aspect of it? Answers to those questions can give you a sense of direction. There isn't a quick and easy catch-all answer on how to get started in event planning, though. A lot depends on you and what you can bring to an event. Not one single event type is good for every event planner.

Some may be good at planning weddings, while you may be better at planning a different venue. For example, if planning weddings aren't something that interests you, there are plenty of other opportunities to pursue.

You may find parties, corporate events or charity fundraisers ignite that passion you need to be a successful event planner. Simply put, you don't have to be an event planner for every type of event to hang your shingle for your event planning business.

Being an *event planner* is a very satisfying and fulfilling career. You just have to be honest with yourself about what types of events you're going to enjoy planning before you get started.

Planning the details for an event that will make a difference to a person or organization means you are an important part of making it special and memorable!

Dear, truly there is something amazing about watching an event go from that first meeting with your new client, to date on your calendar, to an idea in your head and a perfect memory for you and the guests the night of the event. It is an experience most people in other careers never get to enjoy. You certainly won't hear an event planner says s/he had a boring day!

If being an *event planner* is a business you want to pursue with the needed passion, your goal is to stay in it for a very long time. Also, since organizational planning is a diversified industry, you cannot avoid **competition**!

Therefore, you need to be competitive, in a healthy way, to have a staying power. Your selling power is the test of how good you are in your chosen field. Being well-known is not enough to let other people know what an expert you are - this is just one aspect that will help you get customers but your time can be restricted.

Lest I forget, let's quickly discuss some of the things healthy competition can bring to our event planning business:

- *Healthy competition help us to be focused, bringing out the best creativity in us and also broaden our knowledge.*
- *It makes us work harder.*
- *It makes us stand strong even when we face*

*challenges (but before this happens, one must have gone for trainings, seminars etc)*

- *It makes us work closely with people of like minds in the industry.*
- *It makes us identify our weaknesses and strengths.*
- *It makes way for creative thinking.*
- *It makes us work smarter.*
- *It makes us seek for knowledge voraciously and at all cost.*
- *It spurs you to deliver quality jobs and products and looking for ways to improve as well.*
- *It gives rooms for personal and cooperate development.*

If you have been in the industry for quite some time, then some people work for you and help you with all the planning and coordinating events or parties for your company and your team depends on you for their jobs and survival. Having a good business perspective will keep your people employed. What do you have to do to keep keeping up? There will be various and varying expectations from your clients and your employees and a good manager needs to prove your company's worth.

As an events director, you, already, are familiar with the in and out of business. You already know what qualities a good event manager should possess at all cost-

nevertheless, is that sufficient to keep you in business? Alternatively, is there an essential thing you need to consider to make sure everybody working with you is happy?

Your managing skills do not end in being the owner of an events company. You are building a new career for yourself and other people on your payroll. Their future in the business depends on you.

**YOU MAY WANT TO CHECK YOUR MARKETING STRATEGY.** How broad is your span of service? Is it enough that you are doing specific events and finish there?

If you are just doing corporate functions, you might want to consider other options. Do not focus on the usual and start thinking out of the box – don't be static, be dynamically and upwardly mobile, this business of organizing, planning and executing events is fast growing. You have to be ready at all times for the change that can take place and is even taking place. You can find opportunities that will make your business stay progressive as you make frantic efforts to be proactive too. You may not want to deal with expansion, but your main goal is to remain in the competition.

There are boundless choices, hence do not fix your mind on the typical. Consider time variations. Some changes take place almost every day, so you have to survive with the change. Try to cover other events you have not done before. Aside from the challenge, small events like weddings, children's party and the like is one way of reaching out to more people to hire your services. The thought might be new to you, but if you are an experienced event planner, it's impossible not to pull it off.

You have employees who can help you run the show. You can tap their potentials and let their creative mind work. For sure there are people under you who would like to have the chance to work with you side-by-side. You can even mentor employees, which is another way of keeping them loyal to you.

**DISCIPLINE AND SELF CONTROL:** These two qualities are very important of anyone who wishes to be incharge of Event Planning business. Though, considering the two words, I find it hard to separate individually. So many instances where an event planner may have to display his or her discipline and self control attributes, but these abilities should actually show through throughput his/her whole career.

**CHANGE! CHANGE!! CHANGE!!!** Change the way you think, act, relate, respond, react, review, evaluate and enumerate, expanciate, reply all emails and enquiries, behave and carry yourself…..CHANGE! The only thing that is constant is change itself. If you want a better deal, CHANGE for better. Everybody can't be wrong with your personality and way of life which is adversely affecting your business!

## How To Be A Successful Event Planner and Vendor

The current trying economic times are providing the perfect opportunity for many
to tap into their entrepreneurial spirit to effect positive change in their lives while
doing something that they love.

*Event planners* can specialize or can do a little bit of everything. Some would prefer selecting a niche such as weddings, corporate events, birthdays, etc. and you should do whatever works for you. Others may start off planning all kinds of events and then specialise as the business grows.

For many either because of the loss of a job or the realization that they can no longer waste any time working at a job that does not give them a sense of fulfillment, event planning careers may be something to consider.

If you wish to become your boss and become a success at event planning, here are a few tips to remember:

- Event planning may be the right career for those looking to write their checks and is also a great home based business for those who wish to have a career without depriving the family of their time and presence. For the person with the right personality, event planning can enable them to make their wildest dreams come true.

- Event planners can specialize or can do a little bit of everything. Some would prefer selecting a niche such as weddings, corporate events, birthdays, etc., and you should do whatever works for you. Others may start off planning all kinds of events and then specializing as the business grows.

- While verbal agreements can work and some may even stand up in court, a well written contract is a better option in all business transactions. As an event planner, contracts will be necessary when a band or DJ is hired, for a caterer, the venue, suppliers, etc. A contract will usually detail what is expected of all the parties who have entered into an agreement. A contract will help you protect yourself in case the terms of the agreement are not fulfilled.

- Good and reliable suppliers are important for a successful event planning business. A successful event planner needs to maintain good relationships with suppliers which will enable them to go out of their way to assist the event planner in planning a successful event.

- Most people usually only go out of their way to help another when they like the other person. Being nice to suppliers is a great way to ensure success in event planning careers. When an event planner can count of suppliers, it reduces the amount of stress in this area, and the event planner can focus on other aspects of planning the event.

While contracts with suppliers are important, suppliers will usually come through for the event planner and his or her event when there is a good working relationship. Building good relationships is crucial for an event planner.

- When considering event planning careers, it is important to determine how organized you are. Planning a successful event requires organization. Keeping all the information you need for the event organized will allow you to properly manage your time when you do not have to look everywhere for the information you need since you will know where everything is.

- Being organized will allow you to stay on top of tasks and though you can expect hiccups now and then, the organization will help you meet every challenge encountered when planning an event. Being organized will also make you look professional. Being organized will allow you to have a backup plan for everything and there will be few surprises, and you will be on top of all the event planning details.

- A huge part of a successful event is finding the right venue. A venue can make or break an event. Some aspects to consider include ensuring that guests will be able to find the venue easily. The location is very important and will help to determine the level of attendance in some cases. The venue should also have an attractive appearance.

- Use Professional contacts: Good quality and time aervice providers. The first thing that you will want to do when planning an event is to make sure that the vendors called upon are up to the game.
- Don't leave out the basics: Plan ahead
- Get others involved.
- Learn how to control your emotions: Nobody will enjoy working with an event planner that is scatter-brained and gets frustrated very easily and easily transfers his/her emotions on people without necessarily respect other people's psychic, reactions,feelings,background,views,idealsetc.So make sure you a good manager of your emotions!

## Building Your Business:

Why are you into this business? Why do you think people engage the service of event managers and what knowledge do you have about the business?

See, people can only make mistake of patronising you once but will only make a decision of patronising you going forward as you can't give what you don't have.

i had found out that three (3) things make our customers come back and also refer us as we come to the realization of understanding our business. It helps us better in our service delivery.

These are:

1. Knowledge of the job/ business

2. Professionalism and

3. Quality

Our depth of knowledge about our business will always give us an edge over competition. It will make us an authority and boost our level of confidence.

Professionalism in its self, will always separate the quack from the original. Many people found in your line of business are quack and you need to be professional for people to respect your business and we need to be mindful of those 3 things aforementioned in our business.

What separates our business from others are our **Creativity, Uniqueness and Touch of excellence.**

Quality of service and delivery matters a lot. Price sometimes doesn't depict quality. It is the output or result that give you away.

Make it easy for people to identify your brand.

We must alway have or develop our **USP** and make it top notch.

You are playing in the same field with others but ensure to distinguish yourself or businesses.

When you render service, you go extra mile to make your customer or prospect happy.

Render service don't Tender service.

Be on top of your game.

Rendering service is putting your very best and breaking the status quo. You give more than paid for. You are right on time and give extra.

Tendering service is working to standard or expected limit. This kill business and destroy relationship. Every customer expect extra. Stop giving excuse that budget cannot accommodate extra.

Also know that new entrants come into every line of business daily. They come with all the resources and power. They can afford to give free things and even give extra.

Always go extra. Your extra is your marketing cost and it will pay off.

When a customer is satisfied. He brings 10 others but when dissatisfied. He destroy and condemn your business and also chase away your existing customers.

Always ask and look for your unsatisfied customers.

Don't ever leave or abandoned any unsatisfied customers. Always make way or room to satisfy your dissatisfied customers.

Finally. Don't be too big to know what goes on in your business. Read more about your business. Do research and learn new things.

Go back to class or school to know more about your business and also training your staff.

Take care of your staff. They can make or Mar your business. They are your partner and not enemy. They are stakeholders and not competitors

Your business can be a passion but passion cannot take your business to the expected height. Your passion must become a vision that has a mission for your provision.

Passion to Vision to Mission to Provision is the reason you are in business. Owning any sort of business often takes time to grow, but building an event planning business is one venture that typically takes a considerable amount of time. The main reason for this, however, is because you are typically working with one or two customers or clients at a time and the way advertising works in the event industry much of the time is basically through word of mouth-an excellent way to the top.

Anyways, if you don't have a degree in business marketing, I have some other suggestions on how to build your business.

- **Use your Business card professionally**: A great way to spread the word about your business is through a well designed business card. The most obvious people that you will be giving your business card to are clients you will be working with. This goes a long way in telling them who you are, where you are and how you could be reached.

- **Use professional correspondence**: Aside a good business card, another good way is to make sure that the public know about your services via:

- *Professional Letterhead and receipt booklet.*

- *Email:* Having a website is also important like www.havilahdecor.com with a professional email services, i.e. manager@havilahdecor.com. Ofcourse, this requires money but setting up an email alias with a good website for your business is very important. (For any advice on this, please visit www.g50concepts.com.

- *Advertise in Newspapers where fellow planners advertise.*

- *Have an Information Brochure* in places where you could be so visible to people and grow your customer base.

- *Register with relevant Government parastaltals*: This shows the public that you are serious and ready todo business with anyone, beit government or individual. Example: **Havilah Décor, RC49408**. The **RC49408** is the registration number given by **CAC** (Corporate Affiars Commision).

- *Bulk sms*: I use www.purposesms.com to send all my customized messages to my clients and well wishers and add more people to my network.You can buy and keep for future use.It gives your client an impression about you that you are serious and responsible.

- *Get a functional, responsive and dynamic website*, Facebook account, Twitter and be socially mobile.

## Why Good Employees Quit

It is incredible how we hear business owners complain about their best employees leaving them and they really do have something to complain about - few things are as costly and disruptive as good people walking out your door.

The sad thing is that this can easily be avoided. All that is required is a new perspective and some extra effort on the business owner's part. You may have falling into this trap before, yet, we can become better seeing the flaws we initially had.

1. **Business owners overwork people:** Could this be true? Majority of us as business owners fall into this web! Nothing burns good employees out quite like overcrowding and overworking them. It makes them feel as if they are being punished for great performance. Overworking employees is also counterproductive. If you must increase how much work your talented employees are doing, you'd better increase their status, wages, and remuneration as well so they won't go away if the work suffocates them. If you simply increase workload because people are talented, without changing a thing, they will seek another job that gives them what they deserve. You yourself can imagine how much you pay your employees considering the work they do for you!

**2. They don't recognize contributions and fail to reward good work:** It's easy to underestimate of a pat on the back, hug, kiss, praise, accolades etc especially with top performers who are intrinsically motivate. Everybody likes kudos, none more so than those who work hard and give their all. Business owners need to communicate with their people to find out what makes them feel good- for some, it is a raise, for others, public praise, some a sincere hug- and then to reward them for a job well done. With top performers, this will happen often if you are doing it right.

**3. Business owners don't care about their employees:** More than half of people who leave their jobs do so because of their relationship with their boss. Smart companies make certain their managers know how to balance being professional with being human. These are the bosses who celebrate an employee's success, emphatise with those going through hard times and challenge people even when it hurts! Bosses who fail to really care will always have high turnover rates. It is impossible to work for someone 8hrs a day when they aren't personally involved and don't care about anything other than your profit, production yields, business at the expense of their welfare.

**4. They don't honour their commitments**: Making promises to people, places you on the fine line that lies between making them very happy and watching them very happy walk out the door. When you uphold a commitment, you grow in the eyes of your employees because you proof yourself to be trustworthy and honourable. But when you disregard your commitment, you come across as slimmy, uncaring and disrespectful. Afterall, if the boss doesnt honour his or her commitments, why should everyone else? Why should all employees stay then? Why should you still be in business? And

**5. Business owners hire and promote the wrong people:** I hate this with great passion! Good, hardworking employees want to work with like-minded professionals. When business owners don't do the hard work of getting good people, it is a major demotivator for those stuck working alongside them and promoting wrong people is even worse. Some tend to promote, praise applaud those who are professionals in eye service becos they are too far to monitor how each and everyone is doing with them. We sure have professional eye service practitioners in all spheres and we need to really identify them so we won't be busy promoting wrong people! We promoting wrong people is killing and killing our business, no wonder good, talented people leave!

# Chapter 6

# Event Coordination

An event can be a day one would like to remember, but this can only be if it has been well planned and coordinated. Those who have wedded have said that their wedding day is the greatest day of their lives. Despite this, some of the minor things that may have been ignored can cause much havoc and dissatisfaction, some of which can be long-lived. One may not want to imagine what would happen if during the d-day, the photographer or the driver does not turn up. Another tragedy can be if another group had already booked the venue that had been planned for.

An *event coordinator* does the work of organizing and coordinating public or private events, appearances, and events. This entails organizing participants, securing appropriate venues, notifying those who may attend and organizing them, acquiring the relevant tools, equipment, and materials and finally to organize and delegate duties to those assisting him or her during the day of the event. On the other hand, the *event planner* also referred to as the *event consultant* is the mediator, the money manager, and the facilitator.

Meanwhile, there are several character traits that a planner should have posses. Obviously, he or she should *be patient* and calm even when things seem to be going asunder. He, also very importantly, should be a good *negotiator* as he would be the one who does all the orders and the purchasing on behalf of the bride and the bridegroom such as buying the gown and the other attire, get the catering team, hire the venue, musicians, public address system, photographers and so on.

This is because only the best is required but at the cheapest rate. He must also be somebody who can *network*, meaning that he or she handles people and issues differently at the same time. A good planner should also be one who has a sense for proper fashion, which includes the colour, the flowers, the music and the clothing. It would be so embarrassing if there were no colour coordination in the clothing or the flowers and the decorations.

The event planners must be prepared to *work for long hours* especially just before and during the event which may include much traveling and moving up and down to make sure that the purpose of the meeting is achieved. Therefore, the first thing that the planners need to know is the nature and the purpose of the meeting. That would then motivate delegates or the audience. All the work ranging from bookings, reception, stationery issuing, vehicle parking, accommodation, decorations among others should be done focusing on that aim. No matter what the reasons for organizing an event are, every detail must run as smoothly and as close to budget as possible. Every planner or coordinator should have as its mission to make their guests feel comfortable and unburdened as they enjoy these functions.

Good events planners should have the reputation of service, quality, and reliability. Attention to details is another trait for a professional service. Their business is to know what best fits into each venue and how to bring about customer satisfaction. They have the expertise and experience to uphold your company's good name. People can tell when quality planning has taken place versus just another sloppy, hurried or less than perfect job.

An event planner will also have immediate and intimate access to the planning market and viable vendors. This fact alone will go a long way to help you stay within your budget. One of the ways this shows itself is by being in touch with your planning business resources which will allow the clients obtain the best value for their money. An inexperienced planner is often taken advantage of by unscrupulous marketers and charlatans. Many are only out to gouge the unknowing client who has simply assigned the function of planning to an inexperienced "planner". But the opposite of all of these positives is the all-important negative aspect of not using a planning service. There are many things which could go wrong within the time-frame of the function itself. An experienced planning service will probably have already uncovered such dangers and can help avoid them at your functions.

Businesses are becoming more and more aware of the fact that relationships can be more effectively built with the help of regular functions and so, planners have swell times to smile to the banks!

Planning for corporations is not considered professional party planning. It may look like a party, but it's so much more. The goal is what the function is all about and whether it was achieved. The real work is all about the professional details which led up to a successful time.

Do you know what? Event Management is considered to be an upwardly mobile and dynamically sunrise industry today. The industry is growing dynamically due to the sudden gush in Live Entertainment Shows, corporate events, exhibitions, carnivals, festivals, seminars, and conferences etc. The industry started with the multinationals poured into the global market in the late 80s. Today, industry segments like music, sports, culture, fashion shows, award ceremonies and cultural gatherings etc, have become the fundamental growth drivers in the event management sector.

Events are considered to be a power tool for marketing, advertising, promotion and communications mix for all companies, clients and peoples. It has become the most significant part of any marketing strategy. A large number of companies are looking forward to good event management companies or individuals as a means of building a brand image for them. This calls for a demand of event management companies like your own in this sector.

These companies require specialization in planning, visualization, creativity and venue management. Personnel of these companies should be skillful, talented and creative to organize and execute any private or public event.

If you are willing to earn big and live big, then event management career is the right option for you. Don't sit in the corner of your room and ask yourself, *'how to start an event management company,'* rather ask yourself, *'when should I start learning and practicing event management?'*

Learning and practicing simply involves learning and understanding the basic concept, fundamentals, and benefits of starting this company. You can get into event management by joining a firm that will help you gain experience and learn client specific requirements. After a year or two, when you feel, you have gained enough of understanding and experience of the industry, you can go ahead and open the veil of your future for name and fame.

## An Incredible Event Manager.

This is a person who has:

- **Passion**

*Event management* can be a thankless job - often tiring, demanding, stressful, frustrating - so a great event manager must have the passion and zeal to overcome any obstacle to delivering an incredible result. They must have the willingness to do whatever job needs to be done to get to the end point and the desire to create an exceptional experience for both client and guests.

But this passion needs to be controlled. If a sales team comes to you with an idea for an event that they love, but they've already sold the idea and the look of the event to the client, then this can cause problems for any event. Because this rush of blood to the head, this passion, can blind direction.

Likewise, someone managing an event has to turn their passion into focus to ensure all event details are covered off - matching budget with expectation and communicating what can realistically be delivered at showtime.

- **Creative Approach**

You can't develop a memorable solution without abundance of creativity. Once the client provides the idea, it's over to the coordinator to turn this into something amazing. And every event has to be approached from scratch - as if unique. A great *event manager* will treat each event as new, keen to stamp his or her creativity on the event.

Thinking outside the box is the modus operandi of any decent event manager. Just because something has always been done a particular way doesn't mean it should still be done this way in the future. Risks have to be taken, and great event managers have to be bold.

- **Strong Organizational Skills**

A successful event requires incredible organizational skills. Think about the hundreds of different elements that contribute towards the end goal - an event that sends a tingle down your spine and leaves a smile on your face. Multi-tasking is the *event manager's* best friend - from schedules to people, vendors to everything else.

What's more, *the many elements of an event are often changing.* It's a moving feast of adaptations, sudden issues, and last-minute changes - *any great event manager must be flexible, resourceful and capable of being comfortable with a scenario that may never be what it initially seemed, and of course respectful to all involved!*

- **Fantastic Interpersonal Skills**

They must also be an excellent communicator. Events rarely involve a single person or group but a cluster of production professionals with different backgrounds and skill sets, all managed by one coordinator. Friendly, approachable, professional, patient, charismatic - all interpersonal traits that *every manager* needs to succeed in pulling together that big event.

At the end of the day, events are all about people. And that ability to connect, build and grow lasting relationships with the people combining to create your event is something that every manager needs to develop and improve upon, no matter what stage in their career they're at.

Without these four listed top qualities, event management could become a burden or a chore. But with them, once the day is over and the event is done, when people can't stop talking about it and you know you've delivered something special, then all you can think about is the next event, and this feeling never fails to make you smile.

## Benefits of Event Planning Training

Event planning is a vast industry, and many people are associated with it nowadays. *Event planners* have taken the responsibility of managing the event of their clients and put all their efforts to make it successful.

Event planning is exciting and fun filled for those who are social, friendly and fun loving; such natured people enjoy their profession as a hobby. As people are becoming more conscious for perfection, the challenge for professional event planners has raised. Every client wants something different and creative in their events.

In event management and planning, trainees get to learn new skills and basic etiquettes about the event planning that help to groom their talent.

- The students who take event management courses are given demonstrations and practical tasks to perform as the part of a study which gives them more confidence.

- Many students exchange their new ideas and special skills while attending the course; that helps them to learn more.

- There are different fields in event management planning, and you can opt for the specific line you want and get to learn about your field.

- People who are not professional can groom their talent and step into the professional field to earn and learn.

- If you are certified, you can be recognized well in the market and can expand your business by being certified.

- You get more job opportunities, big companies in this field hire their staff for assistance, and of course, everyone would prefer to have a qualified person associated with them.

- While taking an event management and planning a course, students are offered internship as part of their study, and this is the best time to gain an experience.

- People who have not done any course might have good taste and new ideas, but these courses teach you how to coordinate and deal with vendors and make clients satisfied, and you learn about marketing as well.

- These courses make you aware of the competition in the market and you get to know your professional rivals (who are studying with you) and their skills which help you in professional life.

  Certification of event planning course gives you the confidence to enter into the professional life.

## Chapter 7
## How To Stay Ahead Of Competition

Do you know that becoming a certified event planner isn't the end of your journey towards a professional career?

Once you're working in the industry, your next challenge is to stand out amongst the competition! There are many different steps you can take to set yourself apart from the crowd.

## 1. You need to seek additional training

Just because you're officially certified doesn't mean you can't continue learning. Look into master classes designed to perfect your skills and take them to the next level. If you've already completed master classes, think about expanding your skill set. Perhaps learning a complimentary art or trade will be helpful? Clients might be excited to learn that you can plan their engagement party and then plan their large destination wedding too!

## 2. It is a MUST to Practice and learn

You already know that the best event and wedding professionals are always learning. There are, however, other ways to learn outside of completing additional training. Keep up with the latest trends by following blogs, vlogs, and other industry-related publications. Consider finding a mentor in the community who can challenge your skills and help you learn new ones. Mastering trends keeps your skills and services in fashion and makes sure you're always evolving.

## 3. You have to Network on and offline

In the planning industry, one of the best ways to get new

clients is by referral. Clients who are very happy with your work will tell their friends about their wonderful experience. Clients aren't the only people who might refer you, though. Other professionals within the industry can recommend you to their clients or business contacts as well. Network using your social media platforms and by attending trade shows to build professional relationships with caterers, photographers, fashion stylists, makeup artists and so on. You don't want to force your business card on anyone, but you do want to get your name out there as much as possible.

**4. Establish a solid brand**

Many event planners work professionally, but they don't necessarily build an actual brand. Whether you're working with a planning company or concentrating on freelance contracts, establishing your own recognizable brand complete with a name and logo can be to your benefit. You'll appear organized, professional, and legitimate compared to other professionals who haven't built a marketable image yet.

**5. Be proactive about opportunities around you**

Sometimes, if you're very lucky, great opportunities will find you. The most successful professionals, however, are those who seek out opportunities for themselves between contracts. Down time is nice, but you should use it to create styled shoots, submit your work to publications, build your online presence, and network. Stay professional and avoid being too forward, but put your name out there and show people that you're ready to work.

## 6. Specialize but stay diverse- don't be Jack of all trades...

One unique way to stand out from the crowd is to become an expert in something. If you're the only event planner in the area that does proposal planning, you'll have cornered part of your local market. Anyone looking for that service will come to you. But having a specialization doesn't mean that's the only kind of service you should offer. Keep your skills diverse and stay current in other areas of event planning so you can still give clients a full range of services.

## 7. Building a positive reputation

Even something as simple as your attitude toward clients can help to set you apart from the crowd. Being professional is important, but if you're friendly, approachable, and fun to work with, you'll build a reputation for giving clients positive experiences. Clients who enjoyed your company AND your skills will refer you to their friends and write more positive reviews about your services, which means more clients for you!

## 8. Be innovative and proactive

Remember that most of your clients probably aren't professional event planners. Even those who want simple events with classic style will be drawn to you if you can show them a mix of what they're looking for and the truly creativity you're capable of. Displaying your most innovative or unique events alongside your fundamental skills shows clients that you're well rounded. This will impress them more than planners who only ever display pictures of events that are safe and trendy, even if that's what a client will choose.

**9. Show them you're worth it**

Standing out from the competition isn't about showing why you're better than everyone else. Try to rise above constant comparison. You want to show clients why you're talented and valuable in your own right. By investing time and effort in your own knowledge and skills, you're investing in your professional career and therefore a better future in event planning!

# Healthy Competition

Have you ever thought that marketing your small business would be easier without competitors? The truth is that most of us have thought that way. Whilst you shouldn't be fixated on your competitors, you can't afford to ignore them. When there are plenty of jobs and business to go around we tend to get complacent and fail to do the things we need to do to stay competitive. We tend to take customers and employers for granted. Customer service drops off and innovation goes by the wayside.

Having competition is healthy and you would find the following reasons useful.

### It Makes Your Customer Service Better

When you're on the treadmill of a business boom there simply isn't enough time in a day to stop and really evaluate every single customer. While others are getting all the customers, you have ample time to evaluate and appreciate every customer. Make customers fall in love with you and treat them right. Then when competition comes along they won't even think of going anywhere else.

### Innovation Is Fostered

Innovation is important to you and your company because competition makes you constantly innovate. When your business is number one or the only one, innovation tends to be ignored. Innovation is incredibly important and is woven into the fabric of what great businesses do.

### Identifies Your Strengths and Weaknesses

You may not always know what your strengths and

weaknesses are until your competition points it out. Competition helps narrow your focus a little and concentrate on what you're really good at that your competition isn't.

## Competition is good For Consumers

Competition is not only good for your business, it's good for consumers. This is so because consumers get the opportunity to pick and choose who gets their money, time and attention.

## Reminds You to Focus on Your Key Customers

Competition reminds you every now and then to focus on your key customers. After all, they are the reason why there is more cash inflow. By focusing on them you also come up with ways to serve them better.

## Provides the Opportunity to Serve

Indeed when you have various customers you have a huge task to always serve. Competition makes it very mandatory to keep serving and seeking new ways to serve your customers.

## Makes Way for Creative Thinking

Because you have a mandate to always give your clients a

run for their money, competition makes you to put on your thinking cap for better ways to add value. Creative thinking forms the bedrock of any success-minded brand.

### Helps identify potential threats to your business

You are able to learn from other competitors what works and what doesn't. By learning this you will be able to decipher what plans and strategies or even products would be detrimental to your business.

### Helps Your Strength and Weaknesses

You are enabled to study your strengths and weaknesses. Your weaknesses help you become better, while your strength drives you harder to achieve more.

### Stops complacency

Competition automatically pushes you out of your comfort zone because of the quest to serve better. Leaving your comfort zone also helps you to strive to beat the records of your competitors.

### Consumers benefit from competition

When there is competition amongst brands, consumers benefit from through the promotions or other good things that could capture the consumers.

## Helps Grow Your Business and Market

Strong competition can actually help your business because they keep you on your toes. They also provide valuable market insight, and force you to keep your product strategies fresh.

## Provides an alternative for customers who are not a good fit for your business

There are very difficult customers whom you just cannot please. Trying to fit them into your plan could end up frustrating; so you have the choice of leaving such customers to your counterparts to deal with.

## Provides ideas you can adapt for your products or services

You can learn from what your competitors have put in place to adjust your plan. You are also able to draw inferences from the way they run their businesses, plus their products and services.

## Allows for working together on common industry or market issues

When a brand isn't monopolized, there is the ability to form a regulating body in that industry. This is so important because this body is able to serve as watch dog for those who might be defaulting in certain areas.

## Helps You Work Smarter

You cannot afford to work at a snail rate when you are in competition. When there is competition you must be up and doing and to speed at all times.

## Makes You Seek Knowledge Voraciously

When in competition one of the ways to always come out tops is reading and researching voraciously. When you read and research widely you will be abreast with issues.

## It Gives Room for Learning

Learning new things from your counterparts is a sure banker. You would learn to broaden your horizon and at the same time add to the growth of your brand.

## It Improves Your Employees

There is always something new to learn in an industry full of competition. Your employees have a whole lot of experiences to learn from. Experiences like; how to handle customers when there is business boom and how to deal with situations when your competitors have more customers than you do.

**Ability for Development**

All the experiences you garner during this period, becomes a good raw material to help develop your brand. Check the track records of bigger brands; you will see that they put to good use all the experiences they experienced.

Kill that paranoia and begin to glide through your competition rather than feel upbeat. The very moment you become scared of competition and not take advantage of it, you give room for failure to set in.

Failure can never get your brand anywhere. Look up with hope and face your competitors.

# How Best To Charge For Your Services

Today we tackle an important question that new planners often have – "How do I charge for my event planning services?" There are typically five possible ways to charge for your services. Keep in mind that the going rate for fees varies based on location.

## Hourly Rate

Ask yourself what you think you are worth and decide on a set hourly rate. The amount of experience you have will play a role in your decision. A common hourly rate can fall within **$5.5/hr** for a new planner, and go upwards of **$27+/hr** for top event planners with amazing portfolios.

Typically you can charge about 30% more for a corporate event than a social event. Adjusting your prices based on the market you are serving (social vs corporate) is an acceptable practice.

## Flat Fee

Charging a flat fee is the most common and preferred method of billing your client. With a flat fee, there are no surprises to you or your client. Once you discuss the fee amount with honesty and transparency, you and the client can focus solely on making the event as great as possible.

When you outline your flat fee it is normal to charge a fee for your services, plus a percentage based on the total vendor fees.

A standard vendor commission percentage fee is **10-15%** so for example if a caterer charges **$2703** for an event, your fee would be **$81-$122** for locating and coordinating that particular vendor.

The above fee structure goes for both social and corporate events.

In order to protect yourself financially, what I do is it is to receive a **80%** deposit upfront, and the remaining **20%** within (2wks) two weeks of the event or after the event. But, to be frank, I collect all my money upfront most of the time oooooo...lol.

## Percentage of the Event Budget

Some planners prefer to charge clients a percentage of their total event budget. The biggest difficulty with this method of charging is to present it to your client in a way that they will approve it. If you think you can run this by them without the client questioning your billing method then this is a possibility you should consider. Typical percentage amounts are ***15 – 20%*** of the event budget. You can adjust it lower if you feel necessary.

## Day-of Coordination

At some point in your career, you will be asked to do a day-of coordination. These typically happen for weddings but sometimes for special events too. When a client wants to hire you for day-of service, it means they have chosen their own vendors and work with them directly while you come in on the day of the event to make sure it runs smoothly.

You can charge either by the hour or a flat fee for day-of coordination. You should assume 8 – 10 hours of work on the day of the event (multiply that by your hourly rate to get a flat fee), but do not forget the preparation you will have to do. We like to say you should prepare for at least one month to familiarize yourself fully with all aspects of the event you are coordinating. The extra preparation prior to the event may take you an additional 10 – 20 hours so be sure you take this into account when figuring out your fee.

Since day-of coordination events are less expensive for the client, they have grown in popularity in recent years due to a slower economy. So even if you do not anticipate pitching this service, you may be asked for this by a client.

**Vendor Commission**

A minority of planners choose to either heavily discount their client fees or charge nothing for their service, and make all their money by taking a commission from the vendors they hire.

> This method of billing has some supporters and some who dislike it. Those against this method say that you are doing a dis-service to your client by selecting vendors who are not the best at what they do but they will pay you the

highest commission.

Supporters of charging a commission say they still select the best vendors they know, but they just go the extra step to work out a commission structure.

Don't forget to closely monitor your total overhead costs at all times. Overhead costs are made up of all non-labour expenses you have that are needed to put on the event. For example things like additional phone bill costs, gas expenses, hiring temporary help, etc. These overhead costs can be easily overlooked and often make up about 4 – 5% of the total event budget. So be sure to monitor these and incorporate them into your pricing.

Another good approach to it is, charging enough but not too much for your event planning services is key to ongoing business success. It's important for first-time business owners, therefore, to proceed with caution as they begin to estimate the cost of holding events. The goal in pricing a service is to mark up your labor and materials costs sufficiently to cover overhead expenses and generate an acceptable profit.

Fees are typically determined by three factors:

1. **Market segment served**. Social events have a different fee structure than corporate events. In the social events

industry, planners typically charge a fee for their services, plus a percentage of some or all vendor fees. If you were to break down your event planning fee into an hourly charge, a social planner would charge between **$10 - $∞ (infinity) per hour**, plus vendor's commissions.

In the corporate events industry, however, planners typically charge a fee for their services, plus a handling charge for each item they contract. For example, a planner buys flowers from a florist, marks them up (usually by 15 percent) and charges that amount to the client. Another possibility is a flat fee, or "project fee," often used when the event is large and the corporation wants to be given a "not to exceed" figure plus vendor commissions.

2. **Geographic location**. Fees are higher in the City for example, than in the interior villages or smaller towns. This difference reflects the variation in cost of living. In addition, areas of the country with well-defined on- and off-seasons base their prices partly on the season involved.

3. **Experience and reputation of the event planner**. If you're just starting out in the industry, it's reasonable to charge less for your planning services while you gain expertise. A word of caution, though: Don't charge too little just to get the job. Although clients shop around for the best price, a planner who comes in too low with an estimate may be as off-putting as a planner who comes in

too high. Your client may question your ability to throw a top-tier event based on the price you have quoted.

So how are the above-mentioned fees-for-service calculated? Most event planners price their fees-for-service (the total cost to the client) using a "cost plus" method. They contract out the labor, supplies and materials involved in producing an event and charge their clients anywhere from 10 to 20 percent of the total cost of the event, with 15 percent being a rough average.

Before you can begin planning an event, you have to know exactly what your clients want and what they can spend. Then you estimate how much it will cost to contract for labor and supplies, add your commission and present the total fee for services to the client as an estimate. Below are some possible per-event expenses:

**Site rental.** Depending on the event, site rental fees can be considerable, non existent or anywhere in between. This is an opportunity for you to save money for a client on a tight budget. Perhaps a client wants a scenic summer barbecue. A site at a public beach can often be reserved for practically nothing while tony beach-side clubs often command premium prices.

**Vendors.** This category could include a caterer, bartender, decorator, florist, photographer, entertainer or videographer, among others.

**Supplies.** Any supplies not provided by vendors or the client will need to be purchased by your company. This can include anything from food to potted trees to table candles.

**Equipment rental.** You may need to rent audiovisual or lighting equipment.

**Licenses and permits.** Some types of events require special permits or licenses, such as a fire marshal permit or a license to use a musical score.

**Transportation and parking.** If the event requires you or your staff to travel or requires the provision of transport for attendees or speakers, there may be significant transportation costs.

**Service fees and gratuities.** Hiring temporary help, such as servers, for the event can be costly.

**Speakers' fees.** Conferences and other educational or commemorative events often involve speakers.

**Publicity and invitations.** A large event may be heavily advertised, but even smaller events might entail the use of fliers. Invitations are also frequently necessary.

**Mailing and shipping.** If you're mailing out invitations or fliers, don't forget this expense. Some event planners even ship flowers.

**Photocopying** and preparation of registration materials. Any handouts for attendees or photocopying of fliers fall under this category.

**Signage**. Any signs or banners designed for the event should be figured into your per-event expenses.

Once you know which of the above expenses you'll incur, you can prepare an estimate of the event cost and the fee-for-service. First, find out the going rate by contacting three of each kind of vendor and supplier you'll need. Then calculate the costs for each category listed (and any others that might arise), add them up and add a small amount for unforeseen expenses.

When you give an estimate to a client, you may want to present it in the form of an itemized list. Show each vendor or supplier separately, with a brief description of the services they're to provide, and list the price of each service. This strategy is helpful for reminding clients that your company will receive only a small fraction of the total fee for services.

# Chapter 8
# Branding

Let us talk about branding...personal or with your brand!

I would start by exposing us to 7 Reasons Why You Should Brand Your Product and Services. But before then, what is branding?

In every market segment, there are products or services and there are brands. While some products or services exist merely as part of the market in their categories, others have developed and taken on a "life" of their own and have become "synonymous" with every mention of the product or service.

A typical example is what Coca cola has become in the soft drinks category or FMCG worldwide. Eight or nine times out of ten, the mention of "soft drinks" conjures up (first and foremost) the picture of a bottle or can of Coca cola in the mind of most people.

Below are some reasons why you should start the process of turning your services into brands:

- Branding sets your business apart from others: There are fashion designers and there are tailors. Branding is what takes your business from the crowded bottom rung of the ladder and puts it in a class of its own. In the midst of a thousand bottles of soft drinks, you all know a brand that will stand out.

- A branded business represents something in the minds of people, a mind shield, this could be a prestige as in the case of Ferrari, McDonald, KFC, etc. if your business is ever going to have a definite identity in people's minds, branding is the way to go about it. The share of mind is equal to the share of the market!

- Brands are shortcuts to making purchasing decisions- when you mention soft drinks, people's minds go straight to what? Your guess is as good as mine. Likewise, the most seasoning cube is the market is also what? It is a beautiful thing when your brand in the event industry, becomes the reference point, it makes purchasing, using your services, engaging your team, easier.

- Brands are memorable- it is easier to mention some brands than asking for the name of the company that did the decorations, catering, make up etc.? You get it?

- Brands guarantee loyalty- when your brand lives up to its promises, people over time become loyal to it and even act as evangelists encouraging other people to embrace you and your services.

- Only brands can charge premium, because of their premium image. I know of a fashion designer who charges $2 to make Ankara skirt and blouse and some others who charges $20 to do same thing.

The difference? One is a brand, the other is not! If you are a brand, you are a commodity and people who have money prefer to spend it on brands.

- Brands offer consumer safety- once they are used to your brand, your clients are not likely to go about experimenting.

# Chapter 9

# Event Agreement Form: Protecting Your Business

As i come across most event planners as it were, majority do not know that event agreement form is a critical component to a successful event planning business. And while the word *"agreement"* can bring a negative connotation in today's litigious society, having a legal agreement simply forces both parties involved to agree – in writing – to a set of terms and conditions as simple as ABC and the purpose of the event agreement is to protect both parties involved.

Having any conversation with someone and thought you both are on the same page, only to find out later that you both walked away with a very different sense of what was discussed and any next steps, then you have experienced the world of misconception, misinterpretations and miscommunication.

It happens to everyone in all walks of life, in both personal and professional relationships. In some circumstances, the consequences can be small, such as failing to pick up dinner on the way home from work because your understanding was that your partner was handling it. In other situations – particularly in business – the ramifications can be deadly, suicidal, detrimental and costly. Having an event agreement form in place ensures that both you and your client have a clear understanding of the work that will be completed and other necessary aspects of conducting business together with mutual understanding.

When developing your event agreement form, be sure to include these items:

**The specificity**

As an event planner, listing the event planning services that you will be providing may seem like the most obvious item to include in an event planning contract. And, in some ways, it is. However, specifying in detail which services you will be providing is critical as your work will be limited to providing only those services specified on this list.

Event planners perform a broad range of services and the services provided can vary from one event to another. One event planner may provide floral arrangements, another may not. Some event planners may assist with venue selection and others handle transportation needs for guests. No two event planners are exactly alike! Hence, no two event agreement form is exactly the same.

While your event planning services will be limited to those items specified on this list, it is important to also list services that will not be included or provided. Why? It helps you to have these tasks listed in the event agreement form so that your client knows outright that these are services that you will not be performing and basically, the ones you would be doing.

It is also helpful to have this in writing and agreed upon as part of your contract so that, in the course of planning the event, if your client should request that you handle these responsibilities, you have a contract to stand behind when you politely decline to perform these tasks. However, learn to use broad language to protect yourself against performing something that is outside the realm of your agreement upon event planning services.

**Payment pattern**

All event agreement form should include terms of payment and specifics regarding the payment pattern and schedule. Begin with the due date for initial deposit and clearly communicate that no work will begin on planning this event until the deposit has been received. If the event date has been selected, indicate the date upon which the deposit must be received in order to deliver the services for that particular chosen date.

Now, provide a payment pattern or schedule and details regarding future payments, either establishing a set

calendar date for each payment or tying each payment to a milestone in the event planning or execution process. Establish a payment schedule that best suits your business and your cash flow and include any taxes and added fees.

**Terms of Event Cancellation**

Come to the think of it as this questions pops up. **What**

***happens if*** *– at any point in the event planning process – your client cancels the event?* Don't leave that outcome to chance! Your event agreement form should include terms for event cancellation as the case may be. This is an important part of the contract that will protect both your business and the expected income from this event.

Specify that the initial deposit and all payments made up until the point of cancellation are non-refundable. This will ensure that you will be paid for the work already completed. This is critical in event planning as most of the work is completed prior to the actual event itself.

Consider including a clause stating that clients are responsible for payment of any services rendered up until the time that written notification is received regarding event cancellation. This is particularly helpful if your payment schedule is structured in a way that allows for work to be done in between regular payments.

**Termination Clause**

What if a something terrible comes just in time to wreak havoc on your otherwise well planned event? Circumstances beyond your control – such as extreme weather or labour stoppages – that cause either party to be unable to fulfill the terms of the event agreement form are protected by a termination clause, also known as a ***force majeure***. By including a termination clause, either or both parties are absolved from liability in these circumstances.

Be sure to specify the terms and timeframe for termination, such as noting the reasons for cancellation.

### Indemnification Clause ("It's Not My Fault")

Most agreement contains an indemnity clause. But just because they are common, you should not underestimate their importance. The inclusion and scope of an indemnity clause can significantly affect your business. Basically, an indemnification clause provides protection if your client does something that causes you harm or results in a third party suing you for damages. In simple terms, it means your client cannot hold you responsible for any losses, damages, liabilities or expenses that are a result of their negligence. Most importantly, when preparing an event agreement form, do not sign anything until you are completely satisfied with the terms.

### Negotiating? Be Prepared

Before negotiating event contracts, do your homework because once you rush in, you would definitely rush out and eventually rust out! Determine what is involved in planning this event and know what terms and protections you want. Your agreement should reflect shared responsibility so avoid any agreements that are one-sided. What is good for one party is good for the other. When negotiating, be a good listener. Pay attention to contract items that may be negotiable and those that make you uncomfortable. Be confident and do not falter under pressure. Stand firm.

Do not sign anything until you are completely satisfied that the terms are fair and offer you the protection you need.

# How To Appease Dissatisfied Clients

Nothing hurts you most seeing a client with all the efforts you had put in place, yet not satisfied with any of your concerns and efforts.

There are so many things you can do not to allow people spoil your good name and drag it in the mud of irrelevance.

- Dear, simply apologize: when you are in event industry, you cannot escape having dissatisfied customers once in a while. Be wise enough to do everything possible to keep your clients coming back all the time.

- Rectify the mistake where possible: for as long as the two entities involved in a business relationship are human beings, mistakes are inevitable and will often be recurrent. But mind you, they should be kept at minimal level, visit your client or make calls to apologize.

- Empathize, never sympathize with your clients: if you must retain all your clients, then, don't ever assume they will understand with you when you miss it along the way, most especially, when money has changed hands. Identify with their pains and glory!

- Offer compensation or future discount: I will recommend this to everyone who wants to always be in the good books of his or her clients

- Always follow up to ensure clients are fully satisfied. Carry out your due diligence to ascertain that you clients are satisfied as you attempt to appease them.

# Chapter 10

## ...on the final analysis...

One can easily see where event management practice is going and what is involved if done the right way. Even though it is unrealistic to think that everyone should become an event planner or manager...

Always be yourself. Portray the good side of you all the time because of whoever is watching...

Be reasonable in your charges and be realistic in your dealings...

Be prepared for any situation. Sometimes, things go out of control. If you are a team member don't get angry if someone shouts at you, (the person may be tensed up).

If you are a coordinator, do not get tense or panic. Do things coolly. Try to figure out what situation will happen, and what you can do when it happens. A cool mind will produce better results at the right time!

To your success!


I wish you well.

www.ingramcontent.com/pod-product-compliance
Lightning Source LLC
Chambersburg PA
CBHW031432210526
45464CB00005B/2170